LIFE IN CELTIC TIMES

Illustrations by
A. G. SMITH

Introduction and text by
WILLIAM KAUFMAN

DOVER PUBLICATIONS, INC.
Mineola, New York

Bibliographical Note

Life in Celtic Times is a new work, first published by
Dover Publications, Inc., in 1997.

International Standard Book Number

ISBN-13: 978-0-486-29714-9
ISBN-10: 0-486-29714-4

Manufactured in the United States by LSC Communications
297144010   2017
www.doverpublications.com

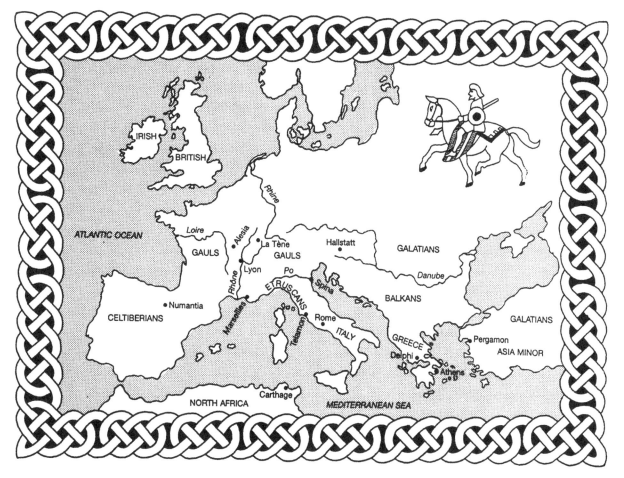

INTRODUCTION

At the dawn of European culture, long before the glory of Greece and the grandeur of Rome, there were the Celts—tribal migrants who spread their family of languages and customs from Asia Minor to Ireland beginning in the second millennium B.C. and flourished until the rise of the Roman Empire.

The Celts (from the Greek *keltoi*) never cohered as a nationality in the modern sense but rather remained a widely scattered group of agrarian tribes that shared Indo-European traditions in religion, language, and culture. They included the Gauls, the Galatians, the Belgae, and the forebears of the Irish, Scottish, and Welsh. As the Roman Empire spread over Europe, most of the original Celtic tongues were eclipsed by Latin or Latinate and Germanic vernaculars; there are some survivors—Breton, Irish, Welsh, and Scottish Gaelic—but their use is declining.

Because the Celts had no written language before their encounters with the Greco-Roman world, accounts of their early history entail as much scholarly conjecture as hard fact. Piecing together evidence from ancient hill forts and burial grounds and drawing on written accounts by Greek and Roman authors, archaeologists and historians have divided early Celtic history into three broad periods: the Urnfield culture (from the twelfth to the eighth centuries B.C.); the Hallstatt culture (seventh to sixth centuries); and La Tène culture (fifth to first centuries), the height of Celtic hegemony before its submergence under the onrushing tides of Roman legions from the south and Germanic tribes from the north. In the early medieval British Isles, a brief summer of native cultural radiance, the Celtic Renaissance, shone in the interval between Rome's receding shadow and the advancing one of the Angles and Saxons.

In classical literature the Celts fall under the rubric "barbarian." But in their rich mythological lore, distinctive craftsmanship, and spirited, stubborn defense of their way of life, they earned the grudging respect of their more "civilized" conquerors and helped to forge the distinctive identity of postclassical Europe.

Hallstatt culture—Austria, 700 B.C. While performing excavations on the shores of Lake Hallstatt in Austria in 1846, a salt-mine director discovered graves dating back to 1000 B.C. Over the next fifty years, additional digs revealed a staggering wealth of artifacts (clothing, equipment, corpses)—almost perfectly preserved by the salt—from the Celtic Iron Age culture that flourished in this area during the sixth and seventh centuries B.C.

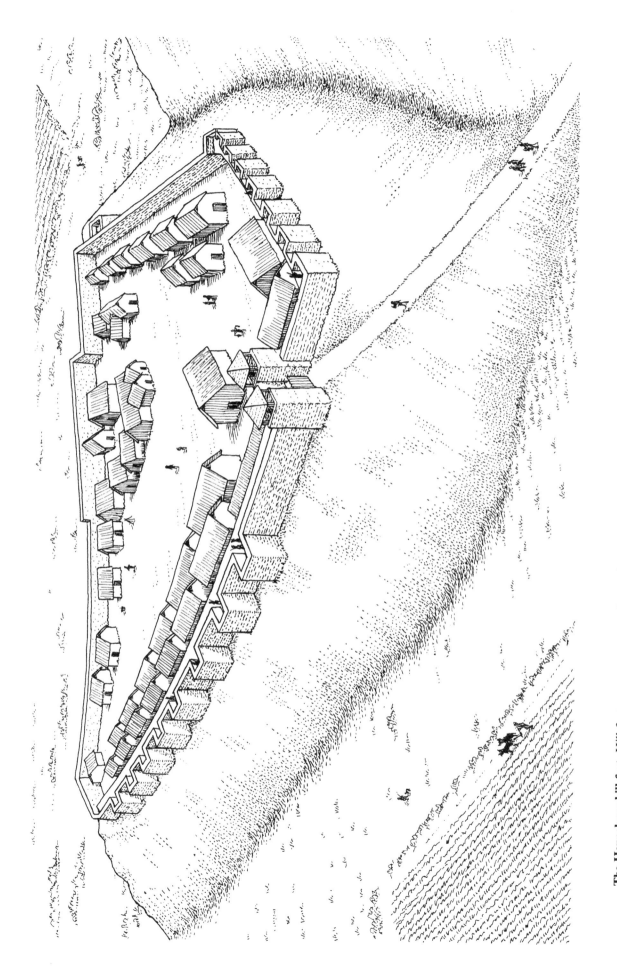

The Heuneburg hill fort. Hill forts were a common form of self-defense for Celtic aristocrats. The contoured remains of many such strongholds can still be seen throughout Europe; one of the most famous is the Heuneburg hill fort in present-day Baden-Württemberg, Germany, the bastion of a family of Celtic aristocrats from the seventh century B.C. until it was overrun in the fifth century B.C.

5

Celtic hill fort—Maiden Castle, circa 200 B.C. Among the many bastions typical of the ancient Celts—brochs, crannogs, and fortified towns—hill forts, hundreds of which still stud the European landscape, arouse the greatest curiosity and interest. Construction projects of daunting immensity and complexity, hill forts were a common form of settlement throughout ancient Britain and Gaul but were rare in some regions, such as east Yorkshire. Some hill forts may have been permanent settlements, whereas others seem to have been seasonal residences, religious centers, or emergency retreats during times of war.

Later in the Iron Age hill forts gradually gave way to oppida and prototowns that anticipated more modern, accessible urban centers.

The dramatic surrounding earthworks still set off the thirty-five-acre central plateau of the famous Maiden Castle hill fort in southern England (present-day Dorset). The fort, occupied from the fourth century B.C. to A.D. 70, was vanquished by Roman forces led by Vespasian in A.D. 43.

7

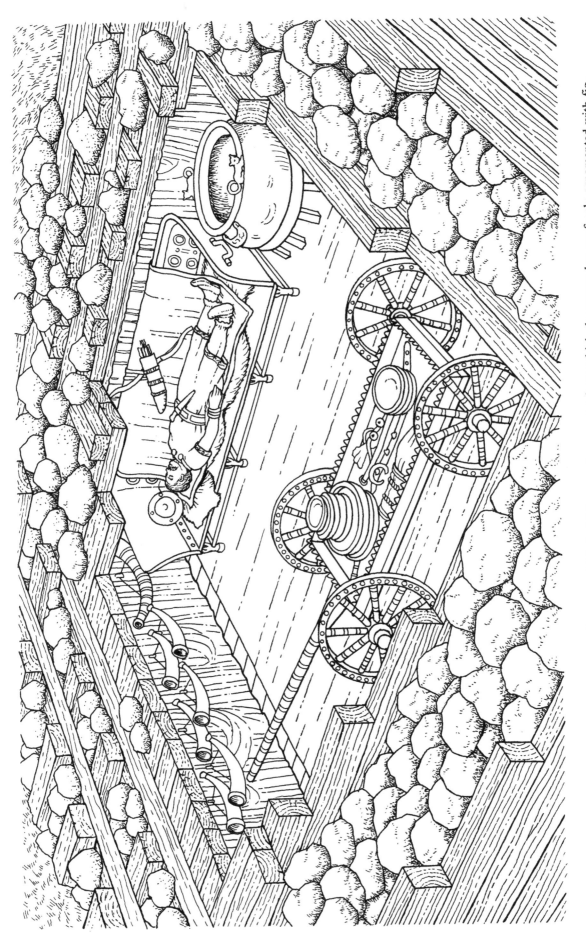

The Hochdorf chieftain. The Baden-Württemberg area yielded additional historical riches in 1977, when archaeologists discovered a mound east of Hochdorf that contained the elaborate, unmolested tomb of a Celtic chieftain who seems to have died in about 530 B.C. Amid the wealth of fascinating artifacts, two large objects stand out: the great bronze couch on which the corpse lay, profusely ornamented with figures of fighters, dancers, and female performers; and a four-wheeled vehicle, perhaps intended to bear the deceased's soul to the next world. It contains enough bronze plates and drinking horns to assure a hearty feast in the empyrean.

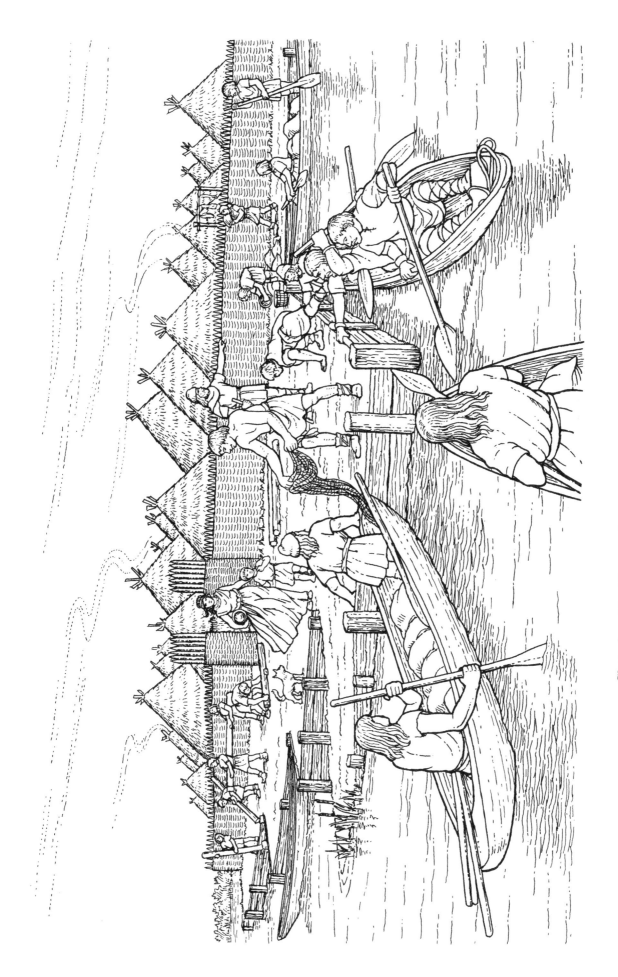

Glastonbury lake village, southwest England. The Celts built fortified residential villages on reclaimed areas in bogs and marshes; the farmers raised their crops on high ground in the area.

9

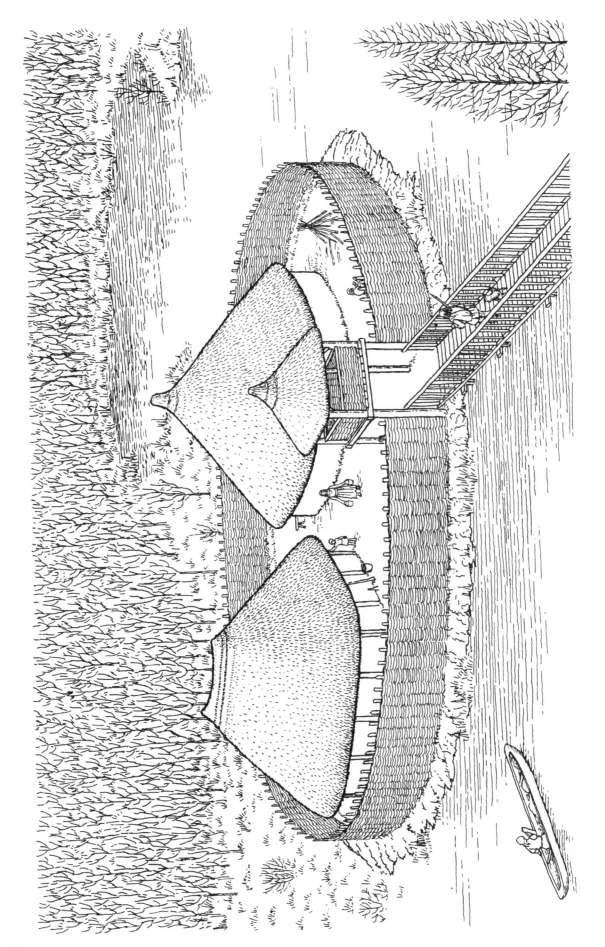

Irish crannog settlement, circa A.D. 500. Ireland is dotted with the remains of settlement sites that range from prehistoric times to the Middle Ages. The settlement depicted here, from western County Clare, is a reconstruction of a crannog, an artificial island built in a shallow lake, possibly as a means of defense. Crannogs, which originated in Scotland around the time of Christ, began to appear in Ireland in the sixth or seventh century A.D.

A **British Celtic house.** Many of the circular houses of the British Celts have been reconstructed, their wooden superstructures having long since succumbed to the centuries. Above the surprisingly roomy interior, a cone-shaped roof transferred weight directly to the circular wattle walls, which were braced and weather-proofed with the application of daub. Where the geological resources allowed, unmortared stone walls further solidified the structure.

Interior of a Celtic house. Celtic houses are of two broad types: the circular structures of the British Isles and the rectangular ones prevalent on the continent. In Britain several houses might be clustered into a closed compound for a single family, whereas continental housing more nearly resembled a village or hamlet. The Celtic household was usually a nearly self-sufficient domain, where corn was stored and threshed, grain milled, bread baked (most houses had their own ovens), and clothing made. Advanced carpentry was a basic household skill, as was pottery before it gave way to commercial production. How much metalworking was done in the home is uncertain, but the extraction and alloying of metals probably required the expertise of specialists who worked for the whole community.

A British Celtic couple, circa 200 B.C. Fragments of clothing from archaeological sites, along with written accounts from classical writers, yield a detailed picture of Celtic dress and appearance. Aristocratic men favored dense facial hair, especially thick mustaches, to complement their spiky manes, which they would often wash in chalky water to enhance their reddish-blond radiance, presumably to appear fiercer in battle. This luxuriant hirsuteness ended abruptly at the neck, however: many Celtic men shaved their body hair, and some Britons even painted or tattooed their torsos a menacing blue. The colder northern climes dictated the wearing of trousers or breeches (from the Latin *bracae*) among the men, a custom that struck the tunic-clad Romans as barbaric and unmanly. Brightly colored apparel was favored among both men and women, especially plaid-patterned cloaks. Aristocratic women often wore peplos-style dresses and a variety of jewelry: elaborate brooches, armlets, and torques, some of which might have borne social or religious significance.

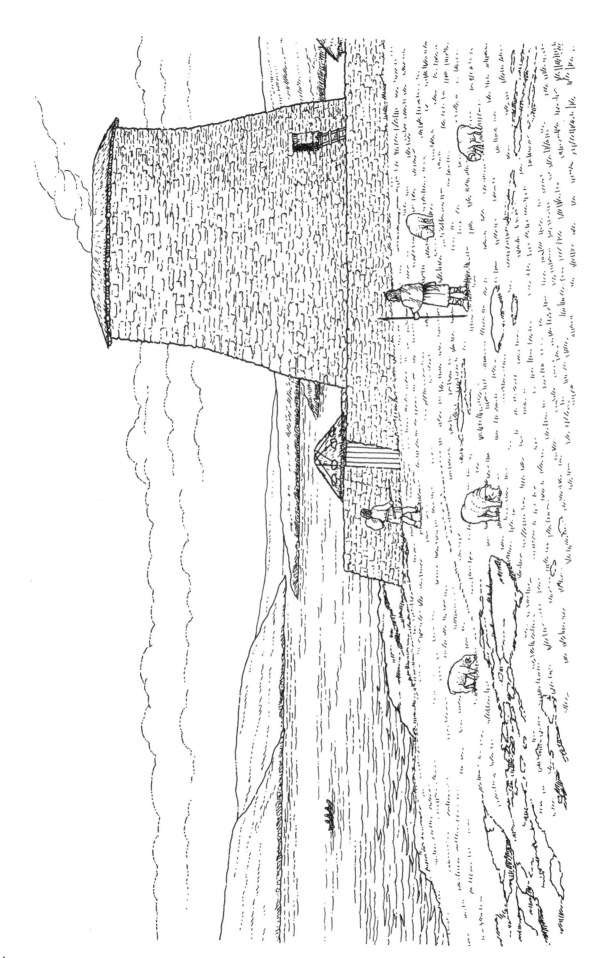

Scottish broch, circa 200 B.C. A common feature of ancient northern Scotland and the Isles was the broch, a tapered, circular defensive tower made of unmortared stone. The broch typically featured double walls enclosing a courtyard. Although some five hundred such structures have survived, archaeologists have not determined if or how they were roofed and therefore cannot gauge their original height.

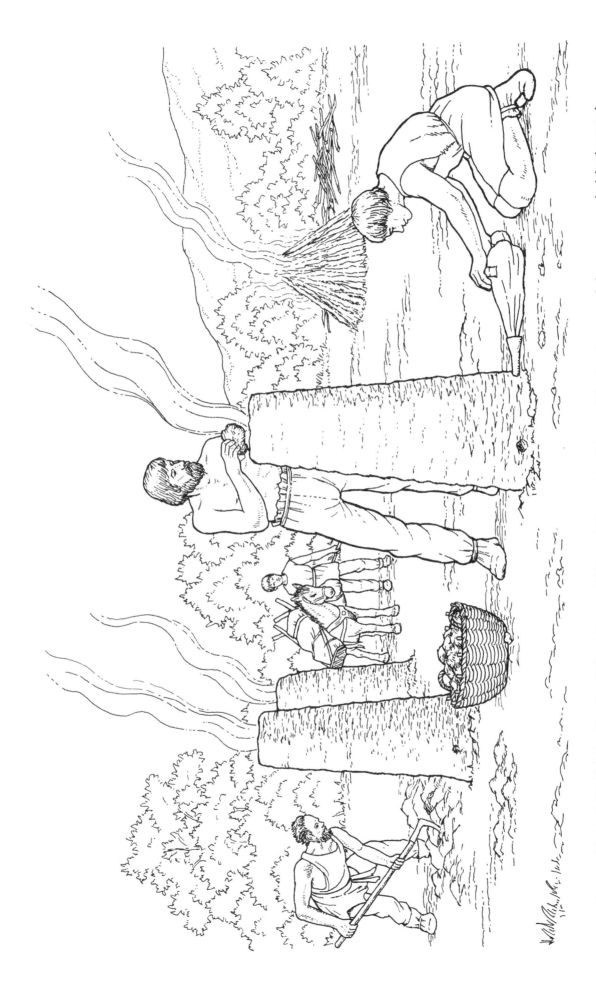

Iron smelting in the Hallstatt region, circa 700 B.C. Between 1000 and 700 B.C., iron—with its greater durability, strength, and accessibility—began to supersede bronze as the preferred metal for weaponry and farm implements among the Celts. Modern simulations of Iron Age methods of smelting and forging have revealed an enormously laborious and time-consuming process, especially in producing mail, the chain-link iron combat shirts pioneered by the Celts and later adopted by the Romans.

Celtic farming—harvesting grain. A predominantly rural society, the Celts of the Iron Age grew mainly cereal crops, especially wheat and barley, although there is also evidence of bean, lentil, and pea crops. Later in the Iron Age, grapes and olives were also cultivated in parts of Gaul.

Celtic farming—plowing with oxen. The Celtic use of the plow in agriculture is evident in ancient furrows deep beneath the ground, in illustrations and carvings depicting plowing teams, and in plows recovered from archaeological digs. Most of these ancient plows were made of wood, perhaps augmented with stone or iron shears. Relying on the simple technique of driving two yoked oxen, the Celts opened up vast areas of Europe for productive agriculture.

Sheep raising and spinning wool yarn. Because Celtic sheep were slaughtered at an old age, they seem to have been used less for meat than for wool and possibly milk. The remains of Iron Age sheep resemble the goatlike Soay sheep from the St. Kilda Islands in Scotland, whose wool is short, dark, and coarse.

Crafts—making pottery and turning wood. Pottery was a widespread and prized craft in the Celtic world. The earliest Celtic pots from Britain have a rough quality, since the potter's wheel was unknown there until late in the Iron Age. Throughout the continent the proliferation of ever more sophisticated designs and techniques yielded vessels of great durability and beauty. Woodworking was also a vital craft, the source of housing, fuel, and products such as metal-bound buckets, lathe-turned tool handles and bowls, boats, and land vehicles.

Welsh coracles—fishing on a river in Wales. Coracles, small bas-
ketlike boats covered with cowhide, were used for fishing on the
small rivers of Iron Age Wales and Ireland.

Wild boar hunt. Hunting was popular among both upper- and lower-class Celts, apparently more for sport and for pest control than for obtaining food. The Celts bred dogs to aid in the hunt for boars (endowed with special powers and ferocity in Celtic iconography) as well as deer, hare, wolves, foxes, and badgers.

Celtic chieftain and driver in wicker chariot. On the farm and on the battlefield, the horse was an essential part of Celtic life—noblemen were buried with the harnesses of their steeds; horses were frequently represented on coins; and, in one unique and telling instance, a Celtic community even carved the graceful likeness of a horse into the underlying chalk of a hillside in present-day Uffington, where that stunning land sculpture has been maintained by the local populace for the past two thousand years. The continental Celts relied heavily on chariots in warfare through the third century B.C., after which time their use was confined to tribes on the British Isles, where Caesar encountered them on the battlefield.

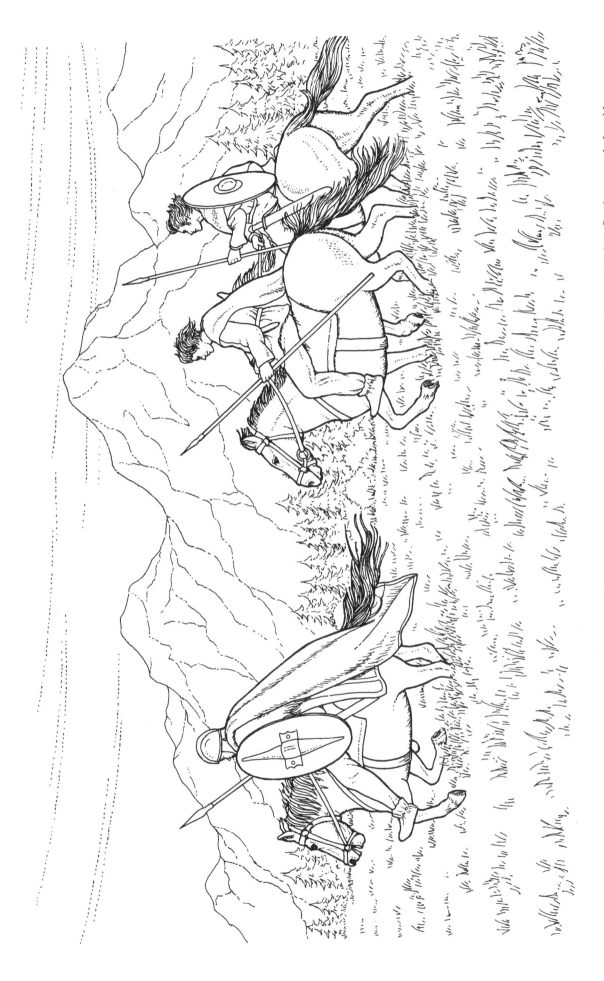

Mounted Celtic horsemen, second century B.C. Late in the Iron Age the cavalry, with its superior mobility and flexibility, gradually replaced the chariot on the battlefield. Even before the introduction of the stirrup, a Celtic horseman could maneuver effectively at high speeds thanks to a saddle composed of four tall pommels that firmly secured the rider. Celtic advances in cavalry technique made provincial soldiers from Gaul and Spain some of the most valuable recruits to the Roman army during the Empire.

Celtic weapons—shield, spears, swords, helmets, slings, and stones. The average Celt charged into battle wielding only an iron-tipped spear and a shield; a sword and helmet might supplement the arsenal of a nobleman. Caesar noted the occasional presence of archers in Gaul; slings were also deployed sporadically, as is confirmed by the discovery of stone dumps in Britain. With advances in iron production, Celtic swords grew ever sharper, heavier, and longer. Shields were typically leather-enclosed ovals of brightly colored wood that ranged in height from four to five feet.

The sack of Rome by Gauls in 390 B.C. Probably because over-population engendered social conflict and land shortages, Celtic tribes embarked on a period of military expansion beginning in the fifth century B.C. After 400 B.C. Celtic bands from Gaul entered the Po valley and continued southward through the Apennines toward Rome. After the Celts plundered Rome's ally, the Etruscan town of Clusium, the implacable Celtic armies routed the Roman army at the Battle of Allia and proceeded to lay waste to Rome in 390 or 387 B.C. (historians differ on the date). Soon rebounding from this humiliation, Rome redoubled its vigilance against the omnipresent barbarian threat.

Iron Age village, Lejre, Denmark. This reconstructed Iron Age village in Lejre, Denmark, is in the area where archaeologists discovered the famous Gundestrup caldron, a stunning silver vessel that depicts a variety of Celtic cultural and religious motifs, including cross-legged figures evocative of Hindu gods.

Celtic religion—the Gundestrup caldron. Found in a bog in Denmark, the Gundestrup caldron, which dates to the first century B.C., is one of the most famous artifacts of Celtic religion. Its strange, sometimes grotesque figures seemingly enact a story involving supernatural beings and animals. In this scene a tribal god, brandishing a magic torque and a crown of antlers, appears in the guise of a hunter.

27

Celtic religion—Beltaine ritual. Celtic religion, a polytheistic amalgam of animistic superstition and ritual (including both animal and human sacrifice), placed special emphasis on the sacredness of various animals, including boars, dogs, stags, bulls, and birds (especially the bird-god Abraxas). Human conceptions of the gods did not arise in Celtic religion until the later Iron Age. Here, at the May Day festival of Beltaine, herds were led between two bonfires in a fertility ritual that was followed by feasting and athletic competitions.

Celtic religion—cult of the human head. Many Celtic tribes revered the human skull because they viewed it as the seat of the soul. By bearing away the skulls of their vanquished enemies after a battle and attaching them to their gates, they believed they were protecting the community by exerting control over hostile forces. The divine power of the human head was enshrined at the Salwian sanctuary of Roquepertuse, with its niches for skulls surrounded by paintings of fish, foliage, and squatting gods or priests.

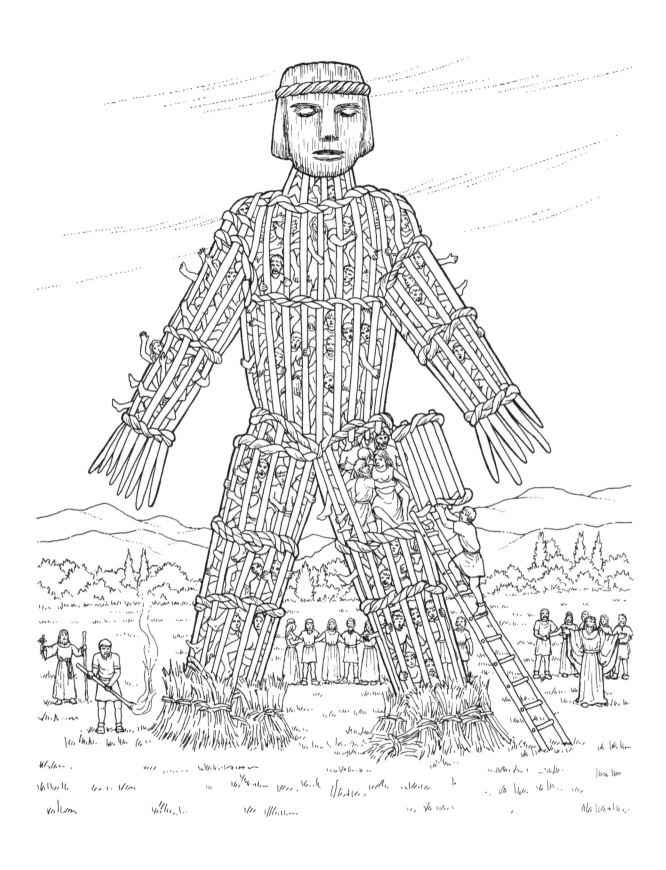

Celtic religion—the wicker man. The Celts believed they could ward off disease and misfortune by offering sacrifices, both animal and human, to appease wrathful gods. The method depicted here was described by Julius Caesar: "Some tribes have colossal images made of wicker-work, the limbs of which they fill with living men: they are then set on fire, and the victims are burned to death."

Celtic artifacts. *Top left:* bronze spring brooch, second century B.C., Switzerland; *top right:* bronze mirror, southern England; *bottom left:* bronze flagon, fourth century B.C., France; *bottom right:* gold torque, first century B.C., southern England.

Celtic coins. *Top left:* Parisii; *top right:* Atrebates; *center:* Unelli; *bottom left:* Dacia; *bottom right:* Danube region.

Celtic artifacts. These bronze figures, which date from the seventh or eighth century B.C., are a product of the Naraghe culture of present-day Sardinia. Note the fierce, otherworldly, nonnaturalistic portrayal of the human form.

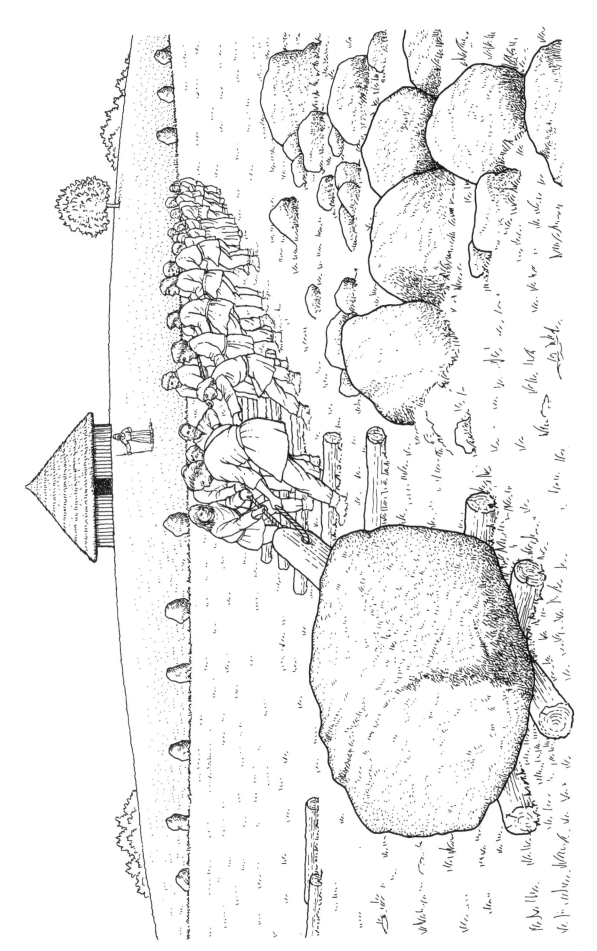

The royal site of Navan in County Armagh. The archaeological evidence indicates that this circular monument, the ancient Emhain Mhacha, capital of Ulster, was erected—with much protracted effort—in 94 B.C., by which time the site was already a major communal center. Concho-bar mac Nessa, the hero of the ancient Irish epic *Táin Bó Cúailnge,* presided at Emhain Mhacha.

Cú Chulainn crosses the ford with the body of his slain friend, Fer Diad. In Irish folk tales of the Iron Age, we have the only record of the mores and ethos of a Celtic people beyond the reach of the Roman legions, an entire cosmogony providentially preserved in writing by monks in medieval Irish monasteries. The central work in ancient Irish mythology is the *Táin Bó Cúailnge* (*The Cattle Raid of Cooley*), which chronicles the life and times of the mythic king of Ulster, Conchobar mac Nessa, and the young warrior, Cú Chulainn (hound of Culann). Cú's epic feats of strength and heroism engender the usual array of rivals. Even his best friend, Fer Diad, meets his doom at Cú's hands after issuing a drunken challenge to a duel; bearing off the body of his slain comrade, Cú laments, "All the fighting I have ever been involved in has been only a game or a sport in comparison with my fight with Fer Diad."

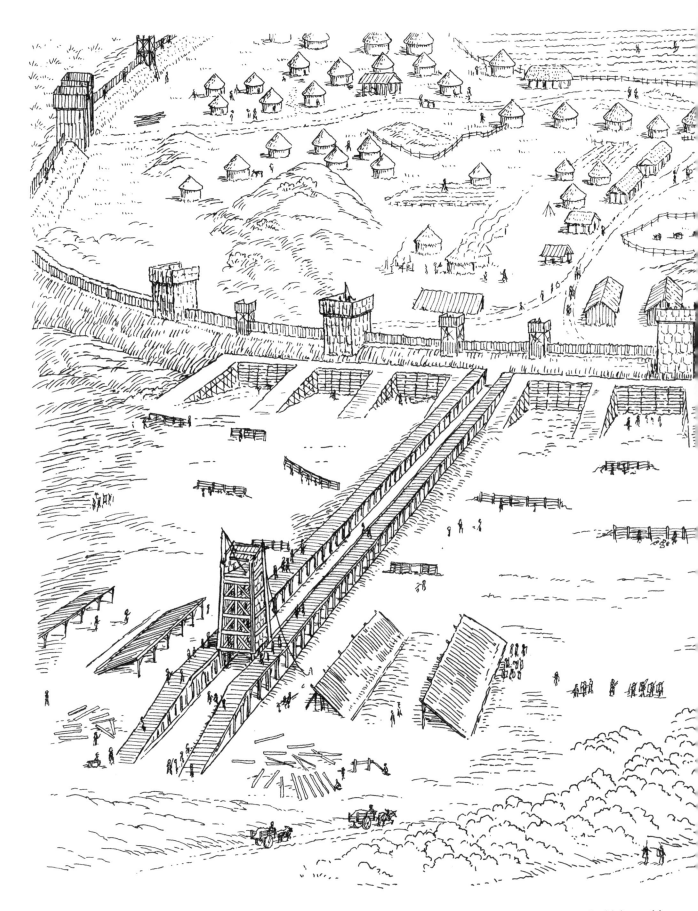

The Roman siege of Alesia. It took over three hundred years, but eventually the Roman army, led by Julius Caesar, avenged the sack of Rome by Gallic Celts. Siege techniques were critical in Caesar's conquest of Gaul, the climax of which was his suppression of a revolt spearheaded by the chieftain Vercingetorix in 52 B.C. Caesar's famous victory there was made possible by

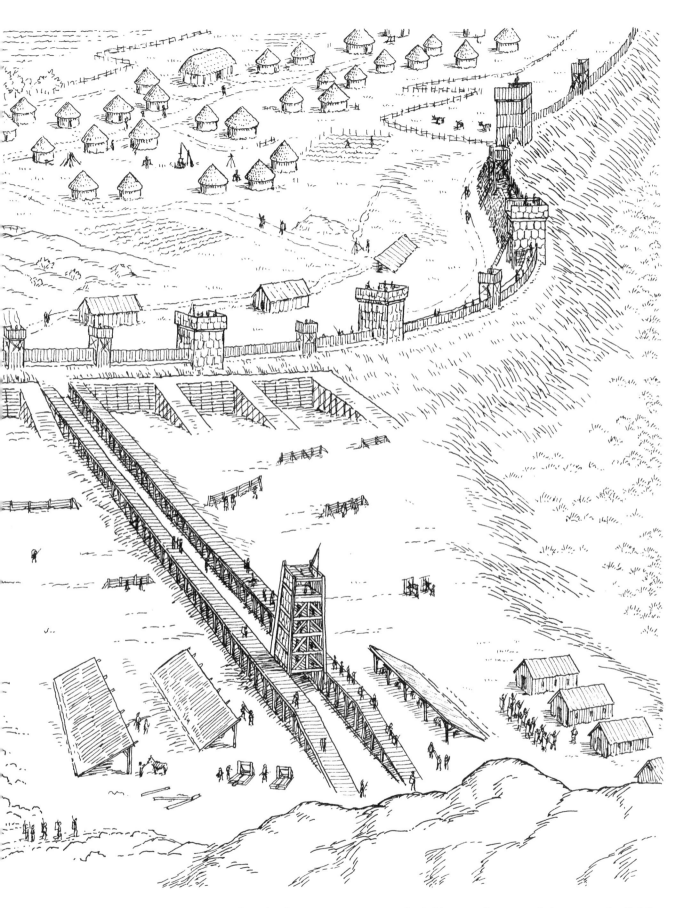

a prodigious feat of engineering—surrounding the fortress at Alesia with *two* walls of circumvallation: an inner ring measuring nine and a half miles around to blockade the fort and an outer wall of thirteen miles to repel the expected relief forces. Constructed of earth and logs, these fortifications were studded with numerous camps, redoubts, and watchtowers.

The surrender of Vercingetorix to Julius Caesar at Alesia in 52 B.C. Trying to avoid open battle with Caesar's armies, Vercingetorix tried to resist the Romans from a few strongholds, one of which, Alesia, proved to be the site of the decisive battle. With his superior technology and impregnable ramparts, Caesar surrounded and besieged the tribal army holed up there, starved out the defenders, and, although his troops were badly outnumbered, repulsed a massive relief effort by a quarter million Gallic soldiers. Vercingetorix was captured and transported in chains to Rome, where he was imprisoned for several years before being paraded in humiliation before the jeering populace prior to his execution.

The Book of Kells. In the fifth century A.D., after the collapse of Roman power in the West, waves of Germanic invasions, vast resettlements, and Viking incursions ushered Western Europe into a Dark Age of violence and insecurity. But for the Celts of the British Isles it was an opportunity for political and cultural resurgence, as symbolized in the exploits of King Arthur and the cultural flowering known as the Celtic Renaissance. In the seventh and eighth centuries, the lamps of scholarship, dimmed throughout strife-torn Europe, burned brightest in the Irish monasteries—most notably at Iona, Lindisfarne, and St. Gall—which also spawned the exquisite art of the illuminated manuscript, in which gold colors were used to embellish elaborately illustrated bibles. One such masterpiece, the Book of Kells, was the culmination of one hundred years of manuscript illumination. Most probably produced at Iona in the early ninth century, it was taken from there, unfinished, to the monastery of Kells, County Meath, for protection from Viking raiders.

39

Saint Patrick drives all the snakes from Ireland. Notwithstanding the embellishments of legend, including the one depicted here, Saint Patrick was a real man who had a major impact on the course of Irish history. Close upon the ebbing of Roman power in the West came the surging tide of Christianity, sweeping over the imperial outposts of Rome and beyond, into the German north and into Scotland and Ireland. Christian missionaries had probably reached Ireland by the fifth century, their influence enlarged, ironically, by thousands of Roman-British slaves captured by the Scotti. One such captive was Patricius, the son of a wealthy British family, who was impressed into slavery in Ireland at age sixteen, escaped six years later, was ordained as a bishop, and returned to Ireland as a missionary in 455 B.C. to spread the word of Christ among the Irish pagans.

The voyage of Saint Brendan. Saint Brendan (b. *ca.* 484, d. 578) is another heroic figure of the early Irish church whose remarkable life story is a compound of fact and legend. Educated at the County Limerick boys' school of the Abessa St. Ita, he became a monk and headed the abbey of Ardfert in County Kerry before moving on to found several monasteries (Clonfert is the most famous) throughout Ireland and Scotland. He is perhaps best known for his adventurous travels, which took him to the Hebrides, western Scotland, Wales, Brittany, and, if the tenth-century Latin epic *Navigatio Brendani* ("Voyage of Brendan") is to be believed, out into the unexplored Atlantic, where he visited many exotic islands and a wondrous land that some later interpreters took to be America.

Early Irish monastery. The Irish kings offered little resistance as "countless numbers" of converts embraced Christianity, even granting land for monasteries and churches. These early compounds usually included a church or oratory, a priest's residence, a kitchen, and, much later on, towers of the sort shown here, which provided protection against Viking raids.

Three Celtic crosses. As Christianity spread throughout the waning Roman Empire in the West, the Celtic aesthetic sensibility infused the newly embraced faith. These three examples are from Ireland: (*from left to right*) Cardonagh cross, seventh century, Donegal; Muireadach's Cross, 922, Monasterboice in Louth; Reask cross-pillar, Kerry.

King Arthur, accompanied by Merlin, receives the magical sword Excalibur. The story of King Arthur originated in scattered seeds of folk memory that spawned a dense exfoliation of legend and poetry throughout medieval Europe. The general scholarly assumption is that an actual king or warlord named Arthur—or a number of men fused in myth into a single folk hero—led the Celtic resistance to Germanic invaders in western Britain in the late fifth and early sixth centuries, a campaign that culminated in the battle of Mount Badon, which tem-porarily halted the Germanic advance in roughly A.D. 500. The chief sources for Arthur's historicity are the ninth-century *History of the Britons* by Nennius, primarily a collection of folk-loric accounts; and Geoffrey of Monmouth's *History of the Kings of Britain,* published in 1136–38, which included an imaginative retelling of Arthur's exploits that helped to launch the cycle of Arthurian romances that pervaded Western Europe throughout the Middle Ages.

Dumbarton Rock, citadel of the kingdom of Strathclyde. Upon conversion to Christianity in the sixth century A.D., the natives of Strathclyde allied themselves with the Cumbrians against Bernicia, a pagan Anglo-Saxon kingdom. The Northumbrians vanquished Cumbria in the seventh century, taking Strathclyde in 756. Dumbarton fell to the Vikings in 870, and in the early 900s sovereignty over Strathclyde passed to the Anglo-Saxon kings of England, who in turn leased it to the Scottish king, Malcolm I. Thenceforth Strathclyde remained a province of Scotland.

Pictish memorial stone. Known to the Romans as the *Picti* ("the painted ones"), apparently for their elaborate tattoos, the Picts are one of the most mysterious of the British Celtic tribes, all but vanishing after their conquest by the Scots in A.D. 685 but leaving an impressive body of stone and metal sculpture. This memorial stone depicts warriors, hunters, and the moon.

Murchad, son of Brian Boru, defeats the Vikings at the Battle of Clontarf, 1014. Through forceful political and military leadership, Brian Boru (941–1014) rose from the kingship of smaller territories (Dal Cais and Munster) and defeated the Eoghanachta septs and the Norsemen on his way to becoming king of Ireland in 1002. The Viking population of Dublin allied with dissidents of Leinster against Brian in 1013 but were subdued near Dublin at the battle of Clontarf on April 23, 1014. Although too old and infirm to direct the battle, which was led by his son, Murchad, Brian nevertheless suffered a violent end at the hands of retreating Norsemen.

Medieval Irish bard. An excellent description of the Celtic bard was furnished by the Roman writer Diodorus Siculus: "Among them are also found lyric poets whom they call Bards. These men sing to the accompaniment of instruments which are like lyres, and their songs may be either of praise or obloquy." The bards were honored craftsmen, trained in special schools where they were intensively drilled in the traditional repertoire. Although pagan in origin, the bardic tradition flourished under Christianity, enriched by the addition of Latin, with its novel metrical challenges. Eventually the freshness and originality of the bardic impulse smothered under formal strictures and rote tributes to aristocratic patrons. Nevertheless, some of the bardic schools survived into the seventeenth century.